The JOURNEY *of* MY EMOTIONS

The JOURNEY of MY EMOTIONS

The Woman That I Am

— JOSIE DORLUS —

TATE PUBLISHING
AND ENTERPRISES, LLC

Published by Tate Publishing & Enterprises, LLC
127 E. Trade Center Terrace | Mustang, Oklahoma 73064 USA
1.888.361.9473 | www.tatepublishing.com

Tate Publishing is committed to excellence in the publishing industry. The company reflects the philosophy established by the founders, based on Psalm 68:11,
"The Lord gave the word and great was the company of those who published it."

Published in the United States of America

ISBN: 978-1-62510-714-5
1. Poetry / Women Authors
2. Poetry / Subjects & Themes / Inspirational & Religious
13.01.17

Thank You

I want to give an enormous and glorious thank you to my heavenly Father, my Lord and Savior for putting the love of writing in my heart. You've blessed me with the ability to think outside of myself in order for my mind to be transformed to serve and help others. Bless your Holy name Jesus.

Thank you to my wonderful parents Zulmie and Jean Marcel Dorlus, I love you. Daddy, you always said to reach for the stars... I searched for Jesus and I got Him. To my brother and my sister who never let me down. My baby brother Jean AKA Lavie Banm Souf, you always pour life into me, by pushing me every chance you get.

To my little girl who is a full grown woman now, my little sister Jerrika "Yourstruly Miss J" Thank you for always keeping your sister's hair fly. I thank God for keeping you sane and safe. My pain subsequently influenced you to want to reach out and touch someone, but we know that's God's job. This too shall pass. Mommy Veronica, my best friend, you are the wind beneath my wings. Your love and support travels everywhere that I go, I love you.

My gift from God, Jayson, my son, my everything. God will use you tremendously and I pray to be around to see it all and guide as much as God allows me. Remember God is in control. Mommy loves you. Jeremiah, and Zahir my precious Godsons/nephews I love you. Salutes to Juju and Macome Saget, God bless you.

Special thanks to A+ media, cousin Loudeline Francois my project Coordinator, Melanie Blair for editing. Thank you to ALL my cousins, and friends who believed in me, and for always keeping on my toes by asking me when is your next project. I love and appreciate you all.

Thank you,

From my heart to yours
Josie

Dedication

This book is dedicated to every woman who's been through trials and tribulations when it comes to relationships. To every woman who has gone through sleepless nights, wondering what she could've done and if she was and is good enough. My women with low self-esteem, with questions, doubts, worries, and confusions, this book is for you. Most of us, women, are emotional. It's not always bad, but when we act on them, they lead us to heartaches and pain.

As women, we need to take control of our emotions and redirect them without causing pain to anyone, especially ourselves. We need to listen to our intuition more often. This gift is a gift that man does not have. So, my sisters of all races, be wise and consult God on every matter. He will stir up that intuition and allow that gift to lead you. Listen to that voice as it speaks to you; shut your emotions down if you must.

I have had some challenging times in my life that could have destroyed me, but by the grace of God, I stumbled, I did fall sometimes, but I got right back up and kept it moving. Some of you have had similar experiences with different outcomes. Some have had worse. Some of you are still going through rough patches, but this too shall pass.

The *Journeys of My Emotions* came about when situations after situations kept occurring in my life. As they were happening, my mind started to travel at times, and as it transformed, there was a decoding process that took place in order to deliver these messages to you. I finally learned how amazing the mind truly is. It's amazing how your subconscious and conscious mind can take a trip together. I hope that this book is a blessing to your life and that you too can go on a journey and learn to direct your emotions in a positive way. Stay tuned for my autobiography book to come.

Blessings to you all.

Love,
Josie

Table of Contents

❧❧❧

Spoken Words

Emotions

Travelling Thoughts

Spoken Words

Is It My Fault?

❦

You showed me who you are
Yet I made excuses
You told me lies, still I didn't believe
Never once you did what you said you would do
And to think that I can change you
What is it? Tell me?
Am I not what you need
Or just good enough to lay with?
I'm talking to you, look at me
You know I don't deserve this
I've done nothing wrong, but put you first
Oh, that's it, isn't it?
It's my fault or *is it my fault?*
To think that you can love me
When you don't even love yourself,
I couldn't see it, but it's true.
You don't know who Jesus is, do you?
Wow, it makes sense now
Why you couldn't have a relationship with me.
You don't know him
No wonder communication was so hard
No wonder why we fell apart.
Oh, God, what have I done?

How can I ask you to fix it
When I never put you in it?
This can't be what you desired for me.
Weak in the knees is how I feel
It's my fault for not consulting you
God, was I too impatient to wait on you?
You did say darkness and light doesn't mix
And here I am unequally yoke
It is my fault because I know the word
Or at least I thought I did...
Obviously not enough...

Josie Dorlus

The Girl with Just a Heart

All I have is my heart to give you
I mean, yeah, I can please you
But it's my heart that has to want you
I'm not bad in the kitchen
But when I cook from my heart, be careful;
You will be a man that is full for days
All I have is my heart to give you
In it, I will hold you.
What comes out of my mouth is from my heart
Like, "I love you," "I miss you," and "I need you."
I may even be too small for you
But my heart is big and strong enough.
What else can I offer you?
When I have Jesus and have been renewed,
So what else can I do for you?
Who else can I be to you?
For when you're down I can pray for you
Wipe off the dirt, quench your thirst,
Break the curse, and even be your nurse,
Console you in every way that comes from my heart,
At the end of the day, all I have is my heart to give you.

Where Is My Adam?

༄

You showed me what a pair should look like,
So I know that it takes two.
Flesh of my flesh, bone of my bone,
Where is my Adam?
I know that you have him for me,
Why is he not here?
Adam wasn't without Eve,
So where is he?
Could it be that I'm not ready?
Are you still working on me?
Help me for I don't understand it.
Where is my Adam?
I can't explain it, but I can feel
That he is missing something,
Something that is in me,
Something he is lacking,
And I can only bring.
The very thing he needs to breath,
It's in me, I know it, I have it...
I don't just have what he wants, but what he needs.
Funny how that is…
What he needs is what I have,
The missing rib…

Josie Dorlus

Bone of my bone, flesh of my flesh,
Together we are complete.
Together we are one.
Together we are stronger.
Where is my Adam?
I know he exists, so please
Let him find me.

A True Friend

❦

Looking back of all the things I had to endure
Some say, "How did you do it?"
Others ask, "What did you have to do to get through it?"
At the time, I didn't know the answer
I used to walk around like everything was great
And when I got home, I would break.
Many times, I cried myself to sleep
Because it was hard to feel the love and everything else
in between.
I remember I couldn't breathe one night
And there was no one in sight.
Or so I thought.
You see, the whole time, I thought I was alone
When in reality, he was always with me.
Just when I thought I was all tough,
He was my strength.
When I had no strength to stand, he stood for me.
Going home to an empty house
With no one there to call my own,
The thing is I was always his; I just didn't know it.
When the feeling of fear would come over me,
He would take me to a place of peace.
My joy was stolen countless times

Josie Dorlus

But every day that I awake, he gives it back
I never could understand how
I'm always renewed in the morning
Singing a new song and feeling alive.
That's because he lives in me
That's why those things couldn't kill me
For he already died just so I can live.
Therefore, in me, he lives.
My body, my mind, and my soul had no choice
But to stay alive as well
The most wonderful day was when we met.
Oh, how can I forget?
I was at my lowest when he picked me up.
I remember I couldn't walk;
He carried me over his shoulders.
Looking back now,
I can only see his prints and not my own.
Then, I remembered that he did say,
"I will never leave you or forsake you."
I was in awe to find someone
That loves me as much.
From that point on, I made a choice
To make him number one in my life.
When the lonely nights were cold
And I needed someone to talk to, cry to,

and even vent to,
It was he that answered my plea
I knew then, without a doubt,
That he is my only true friend.

Josie Dorlus

Are You Ready?

꿶꿶꿶

Before I gave you my heart,
I warned you how it can fall apart.
"Do you have what it takes to mend this heart?" I asked.
"Oh, what a simple task," you said.
"This love is different," you added, "It's kind,
And it can really blow your mind."
"That's the kind of love I need," you replied.
But are you equipped, by any means,
To get through the necessaries?
Are you available to pour out the concrete
And build the foundation that can stand against the wind?
Will you go the extra mile when I'm tired?
Will you love me still when I don't want to be bothered?
Will you hold on as the wind blows north
and we're heading south?
Or will you get tired and float away with it?
So tell me, are you ready for this kind of love?
How will you handle it,
if the opportunity presents itself?

Freedom

He said he had a dream.
That this day will come .
He said he had a dream.
That we will be as one .
He said he had a dream.
That we will be united.
He said he had a dream.
That we will be accepted.
Today, the dream is here.
Today, we can march on.
Today, his dream is real.
The dream is still alive.
Freedom, oh, sweet freedom.
The price was paid just to be free.
Freedom, oh, sweet freedom.
Thy kingdom come.
Thy will be done.

Josie Dorlus

Have You Forgotten Me?

೦ᑉᢐᡳᠥᡳᑉ᠐

You birthed me with a heart that loves to love,
Yet sometimes, it's not enough.
You allow me to go through situations
to build up strength,
But when will the pain end?
I've been knocking on your door
just to hand in my requests,
Still you keep giving me tests after tests.
I know that you're busy mending other broken hearts,
But what about me, and when will it be my turn?
When will you give me a sign of hope?
How long will I have to cope?
I've prayed and begged, prayed and begged,
Trying not to live in regret, and for years,
I felt abandoned and neglected
To know that you said you'd
never leave nor forsake me.
So what happened?
Have you forgotten me?

Thankful

ↄⅇⅈⱺⅈⱺⅇↄ

Jesus, I am grateful
For my yesterday, today, and my tomorrow.
Jesus, I am hopeful
For the vision that you place
In my heart—it will remain
With your guidance.
You raised me up when I was down.
You took an interest upon my heart,
And with the wind, you dried my tears
How could I ever repay you, Lord?
And when I look down at the steps I've taken,
These footsteps are not mine.
They are yours, and for that, I am grateful
For that, I am hopeful
For that, I am thankful to you.

Josie Dorlus

The Color of My Skin

❧

Look at this world today, and how we're living
I ask myself one thing, "Why we cannot get along?"
We are created from the same God above.
We need to love ourselves before we can love others.
I wonder why this world is filled with anger.
When God created us, it was love he had in mind
It makes me sad to see how we hate each other.
We need to stop the hate and just live in harmony.
Unfortunately, harmony is hard to find,
Whether your skin is black or white,
it shouldn't matter
Some say that we've tried, but it's usually a lie
The color of my skin shouldn't matter
Why not just compromise?
Together, you and me
It's not so hard. Why don't we try?
It's easy as one, two, three
Why not just stop the fight?
Together you and me
It's not so hard
Why don't we try?
Make this world a better place

The Signs

When you met him
There was something strange about him
That you couldn't pinpoint
His appearance blinded you
And turned you into his fool
When you met him
And he said those very words
That captured your world
Left you vulnerable, open,
and that's when it all begins
You're on a journey now that's at his command
There is nothing that you won't do for that man
When you met him
And he said hello,
Your heart was the first to jump
Then your head slowly agreed, but your gut said,
"Oh no."
"I can change him," so you thought
"I can be more," and you did
"What about me?" your heart asks
"It's about me," his actions speak
You still can't see it.
"But he does love me," your mouth uttered

Josie Dorlus

"I thought he said it," your brain wondered
"I can feel it," your mind pondered
Questions after questions, still no answer
Confusing isn't it?
The writing is on the wall, my dear
The greatest book says that,
"you will know them by their fruits"
A rotten fruit today will continue to rot
until it's completely dead
And leave an awful smell
He said he cares for you
But what does his actions show, my dear?
If only you noticed it, you see…
Remember that discomfort feeling?
How many times you made excuses for it?
Not following your intuition
Causes you to be somebody's fool
Doesn't feel so good, does it?
The beginning of something should be beautiful,
But if it starts with pain and sorrow
Then, you'll end up with "what ifs"
Trying to cope with tomorrow

The Other Woman

Have you ever wondered why he is so distant?
Have you thought about why he smelled
a certain way when he comes home?
Do you wonder why he has no energy? For you that is
Why is it that you're always half-pleased?
You don't think he says the same things to me?
That I'm the only one that makes him feel that way…
So busy fighting for a title
because your clock is ticking
Wow, that is sickening.
As a matter of fact, you're pathetic, don't you think?
You chose to be naive and
pretend to be happy for society,
Just for people to call you Mrs.
Think about the many times you've smelled me
On his neck, his clothes, and his breath.
But still, you convince yourself
that you're the only one
Am I the other woman or are you?
The world may never know.
He still thinks he's the only man.

Josie Dorlus

Home

When I think of home,
I think of a place that's filled
With pride and such beauty.
When I think of home,
I remember how everyone used to laugh.
When I think of home,
I see a mother that's crying
Over the loss of her children
With hopes that some of them
Will return.
Haiti, oh, don't they know
You were the first among nations
After all that you've been through,
Yet you stand still
With your head up high,
And to know that the day sure will come
When you'll smile.
Oh, my love, *mon pays* Haiti.
Even in the news,
They never once truly
Showed your true beauty,
And it's such a shame
They'll never see

Or will know what you're worth.
How can we forget
What our ancestors fought for?
If they were alive,
They'd be ashamed
To see what motherland has become.

Josie Dorlus

Standing Up for Something

ᥲᥱᠯᥲᠯᥱᥲ

It takes time to realize that we all have a purpose,
Unfortunately sometimes, it takes a
tragedy for us to focus
Your purpose will help you understand your worth.
You will know exactly what to do to make it work.
Believing in yourself is key
Knowing that you are unique
Because that's how God wanted it
When you want something, work for it
For whatever that is easy is not worth keeping.
Aim high and don't settle for less
Don't be fooled by words alone,
Let the actions speak for themselves.
Be firm on what you believe in
Don't let people change your mind
Don't let opinions bother you
and change who you are
Build a foundation and stand on it.
Find your destiny and walk in it
If you don't stand for something
You'll fall for anything.

While Waiting for the One

Get closer to God,
Love yourself a little more each day.
Spend more time getting to know you.
Work on your weaknesses
to make room for strengths
While waiting for the one.
Learn to be patient, and forgive
Take a trip where you've always wanted to go.
Accept where you went wrong and move on
While waiting for the one
It will be hard, but hold on
While you're waiting for the one, pray more
Pray for guidance, wisdom, grace, and discernment
Better yourself, go back to school,
and expand your mind.
Have fun, relax, and do what makes God happy,
and you will be happy.
While waiting for the one.
Keep your head up high and don't give up.
No matter how long it takes;
it doesn't mean that you're forgotten.
So just wait and have faith
that the best is yet to come.

Josie Dorlus

Emotions

Chagrined

I'm sorry for the pain I've caused you.
I'm sorry for the ways that I've treated you.
I would give anything to take them back.
I have learned from my mistakes
All I want is for you to forgive me
Give me another chance,
And I will prove to you
That I am worth a second chance
I have not been the same since you've been gone.
The tears from your eyes were not from joy,
And I'm sorry
I'm lost without you.
Didn't know the treasure I had in you,
Didn't know how good I had it till you left me.
Now, I know that I'm better with you
than without you.
My life has no meaning if you're not in it.
I may not be worthy of your love anymore...
One more chance is all I need
Please, baby, forgive me for I'm truly sorry.

Josie Dorlus

Taking a Chance

ⲟⲉⲧⲟ-ⲟⲧⲟ

You're scared, and I understand…
I've been there before, so just hold my hand.
I know it's new but look at you….
Look at me, look at us,
how we feel when we say I love you.
There is nothing to be afraid of.
For God does not give us the spirit of fear,
but of a sound mind.
There is nothing to be ashamed of…
If only you could comprehend
A love like mine right in your hands
So don't run from it…
Embrace it for what it is instead
Don't run because you don't understand it
That's the coward way, you know
To give up on something you don't know
I know you're scared, so take my hand.
It's time for new footprints in the sand.

If You Only Knew

৯৵৵৩৵৽৹৵৵

If you only knew how much I missed you
The way you were into me, loving me, pleasing me
If you only knew how I valued what we had
When we made promises to love
and honor one another.
If you only knew what it meant to me
For you to be my everything
If you only knew the feelings
that ran through my body
When they called me Mrs.
If only you heard the echoes of my heart
Each time I said I love you
When my lips stopped saying it,
it ricocheted through and through still
After years in the making
and you can say that we're through
Wow, who knew?
To know that the lips that once said I love
you are saying I hate you now.
If you only knew how that made me feel
Angry, sad, lonely, and worthless
You know damn well that's not how it used to be
If you only knew how lonely I've been

Josie Dorlus

When nights went by and you hardly touched me
But all I could do is play back what once was
until I fell asleep.
For the longest time, this dream is on repeat
I just wanted it to end
And here you are, in front of me, you stand
To take away the vows
The ones you thought you meant
But only if I knew...
Things would be different.

My Last First Love

ᘓᘏᘒᘏᘒᘐ

Time and time again, I waited for you to find me
Yet still, I was lost without you
Time and time again,
I dreamed of being in your arms
But far away, you still remained…
Up until the day when I first saw your face
I can remember how my breath was taken away…
The love I have inside of me
gives birth to joy, peace, and hope,
Laughter, togetherness, and everlasting unity…
I knew that I would know when my king arrives
For only you have the magic touch
to mend my fragile heart
I knew that I would know that it is you
For you alone can make me fly so high
Oh, how I love you
With all that I am, all that I'm not,
all my haves and have-nots.
My love for you has no limit, no boundaries
It goes as high as the clouds and as wide as the sky
Some years ago, a powerful man was born
Fully equipped as he should be
Never thought we would have a chance to meet

Josie Dorlus

But fate was on our side
We took a chance at romance
And it's never been the same since then…
A picture of a face was all we had
With just a click, and there we were
On a journey that's unimaginable
We felt a love we couldn't compare
The only thing was left to say
At last, my love is here to stay
Because it feels so good to have you
as my first last love…
Happy Valentine's Day

Moving Forward

I'm tired of living this way
I'm tired of trying to love you
Of all the years I've put in this
I could've been a doctor, lawyer,
somebody greater
I'm tired of losing control over my life,
especially my heart
Something is wrong, but I'll keep on moving
For my day has yet to come
I'm ready to take back my life
I'm ready to take back what's mine
Of all the years you stole from me
I could've been with someone that loves only me
I'm ready to watch you pay, oh…
For all the wrong that you've done to me
Karma does exist; she will come knocking
For your day is soon to come
Moving forward is what I'm gonna do
Looking forward is what I have to do
Staying focus is how it's gotta be
Moving forward is what I have to do.

Josie Dorlus

If I Could Change Anything

I remembered the first time I fell in love
I remembered my first kiss
I remembered how I felt when
I looked into your eyes
I remembered how I was so naive
There was no one else but you
Later on, to find out you're the one
that broke my heart in two
I remembered how I disobeyed my dad
Just because I was in love
I remembered all the promises
you made before our vows
I remembered all the lies you told
And that should've been my cue
But I was in love and blind,
I chose to see good in you
From the moment that we fell apart
My heart's never been the same
Find it hard to trust someone with it
Just because of what you did
Though I've moved on with my life again
It's like you scarred me for life
But I held my head up high

because I wasn't to blame
I've been trying not to live in regret
Till this day, you're causing me pain
Tried to take away the only true love
I have ever known
Though you robbed me of my youth,
and you're still not satisfied
After all the hell you put me through,
you're still in my life
The only gift that I got was my son
If I could change anything else,
I swear I would
The only gift that I got was my son
If I could change anything else,
I'll change his daddy.

Josie Dorlus

None Like Me

෨ඝ෮෨

You seemed distracted by my personality
But I bet you wonder if I got a brain in my head
Didn't your mama tell you
not to underestimate a woman?
Didn't daddy ever show you
how to treat a woman right?
I know it's not easy to find a woman my kind
Frightening, isn't it?
Because I have my own mind
Yes, I am a different breed, you see
I work hard for what I need
You think I need you for your money?
Well, maybe sometimes, but not really
How dare you compare me with someone else?
What do I look like, your mistress?
You can have all the money in the world
You will never know my worth
Nor will you see what I deserve
So stuck on yourself like you can find better
Hmm… I beg to differ.
I'm one of a kind,
that's why I've decided not to pay you no mind
Because a gem like me is hard to find

You've been close, but no cigar
Afraid to admit it, that's odd
Look around you....
I know you noticed that there is none like me.

Josie Dorlus

The One I Waited For

Never thought this day would come
To be standing here before God and everyone
Declaring and professing my love for you
A love that you gave birth to
A love that you inspired
A love that you've nurtured from the beginning
As I prayed and prayed
I knew that when you arrived,
you could only be from God
For there has been many frogs
But you, my love, are my king as I am your queen
Waiting for you was not easy
But with all that I am, I stayed on my knees
For God only gave his best, which is you, my love
My mind, my body, my heart, and my soul
Have been in agreement since we met
So today, I want the world to know that
You're the one I've been waiting for.

It Doesn't Matter

No matter how much I showed you I'm into you,
It doesn't matter.
I made myself available for you;
It doesn't matter.
When you needed someone the most,
I volunteered my time and anything I had
Just for you not to be sad.
I prayed for you, sent you words of encouragement
To see you through,
Still it doesn't matter.
I've reached out to you,
even changed my plan sometimes,
Always thinking of ways to put a smile on your face
It doesn't matter.
When you're down, I felt it,
Tried my best to lift you up,
Still you don't get it.
I've watched you play games;
I even know when your needs are met by others
Because of the way you ignored me or kept it short.
Yes, it bothered me.
To be right before your eyes, and still,
you can't see me.

Josie Dorlus

Does it matter how I feel about you?
Does it matter what you mean to me?
I'm trying to show you that I'm different,
To take a chance,
But I guess it doesn't really matter, does it?

The One That's for You

When you meet this person
It won't matter what they look like
or what they have on.
When you meet this person
It will be an unexpected instant connection.
The one that's for you will make time
Even if it's to say hi
Because the thought of not hearing
your voice for one day
Will make him feel a certain way
Trying to figure out your needs and wants
Hoping to be the one you'll ever want
The one that's for you will love you
But won't know why and won't care to ask
What matters will be being with you at any cost
Your wishes will be at their command
Your happiness will mean so much to them
That they will have it no other way
The one that's for you
will be there even if they are late
Through the storms and the rain,
their presence will be there anyway
The one that's for you

Josie Dorlus

will give their all with no expectations...
Their love and affections for you
will show by actions
When all you have is gone
And their arms are still holding on
That's when you'll know
that the one standing by your side
was always the one for you...

You Robbed Me

I wonder where I would be right now
If I never met you?
I wonder what kind of life I would've had.
You caused me pain over and over again,
Asking myself why did I stay,
What was I afraid of looking back?
I wish I had the guts back then
to do what I thought of,
Dreamed of, but couldn't,
From the first lie to the last.
Today, you still have a straight face;
Only nothing about you is as such.
The nerve of you…
Not only did you rob me, but you shamed me
Before my friends, family,
and everyone else that was watching.
Can you pay me for the amount of times
that you made me cry?
Can you undo the emotional scars that I bore?
Countless years is what you stole from me—
Eleven to be exact.
If only I could cash in for all you've caused
Who knows, I could've been rich by now.

Josie Dorlus

Where would I be? Who would I be with?
How would my life be today?
What I wouldn't have are nightmares
About betrayals, dishonesty, and unspeakable pain.
What I wouldn't have is the fear
that the next man might be just like you.
Oh, what a shame.
And to think that I shared my heart
and my bed with you,
Most of all, a child.
Heaven help me when I have to explain
The relationships you destroyed,
Thank God, that have been restored.
You knew exactly what you were,
but then, you robbed me anyway.
The years you took can never be replaced.
The nerve, you had expected me to stay
And throw away what was left in me.
For many years, I fought through and through.
Oh, the cross I bore because of you.
But I found the strength in Jesus's blood
while holding on to my own son.
You've tried to steal his love from me,
Something that was made just for me.
I tried and tried to forgive you,
But every day, you're still playing me for a fool.

It's a work in progress to forgive you,
But I'll get there some day
Because that's the only way I'll ever be free of you.

Josie Dorlus

Unconditional Love

の～の～の～

There are people who love you for what you have
There are people who love you for what you bring
But there are people who will stand by your side
From the time you have nothing until you have it all.
There are people who just love to receive
There are people who don't know how to give
But there people who will love you through your flaws.
That's unconditional love; they'll be there through it all.
When you love someone, it doesn't matter what they have
When you love someone, you have to look within
It's so simple to be distracted by their looks
But when all has faded away, what do you look forward to?
When you love, you can't have a hidden clause
It's not a contract with an expiration date
It shouldn't have any boundaries; true love has no limit
Unconditional love is the best love to have
Unconditional love is so hard to find
Unconditional love is hard to recognize
People have so many strings attached to love
When it's simple just to love without a cause
That's unconditional love.

Let Me Show You

Come into my world
Let me show you who I am
Let me show how you would
be treated as my man.
It's a journey, brace yourself
Fasten you seatbelt and enjoy the ride
There might be some bumps on the road
Hold on tight, don't let go.
Full coverage, I got you just in case.
Let me show you what love is.
When you're in need of anything
I will be there
I will comfort you through your deepest sorrows
You will never face another tomorrow alone
By your side is where I'll be.
I will be strong for you when you're weak
Even carry you, should you need me to.
I will tear for you when you can't cry
You've had many options, but I'm the choice
Choose me, choose to be loved unconditionally,
Not desperately, but unselfishly
Let it go, baby, don't fight it
Just let me show you.

Josie Dorlus

Love to Me Is...

രാഗ്രാ

The simple fact that I accepted you for you
Being grateful just to have you and no one else
Being able to feel things with you
that have never been felt
Being able to feel your heartbeat
in sync with mine
As they play a beautiful melody in a loop
And to know that my heart is offbeat
when you're not around
Sharing my dreams with you
Being able to read your thoughts
as our hearts merge
To smell you when you're near
To think of you and you appear
To do anything for you just because
To know my symptoms before my pain
To feel your warm embrace
like a blood transfusion.
Love is how I long to be with you and only you
Love is when I'm light on my feet,
As you take my breath away
Love is when you're the medicine I need to heal
The cure to my disease

The air that I breathe,
As you're the wind beneath my wings
Love is what runs through my veins
when our lips meet
Love is the essence of you
To me love is just you.

Josie Dorlus

The Woman That I Am

I can love you with all my heart,
But you hurt this heart of mine.
It will fight like hell to stay alive.
I'm a woman that can turn your house into a home,
A home, a sanctuary, where you dwell.
I'm a woman that can nurture your needs,
Break my back to pay the bills,
Yet still find the time to make sure you're pleased.
I'm a woman, a role model for your kids,
Teach them, love them as my own.
Yes, I have a child, that means I'm a package:
His love plus mine equals a double dose of love—
Joy, laughter, peace, and a sense of family.
Subtracting any of these things and add pain
Will equal to heartaches to the tenth power.
I'm a woman that respects herself along with the king
That values and knows the worth of his queen.
Most days, I'm sweet…
But don't underestimate my kindness, gentleness,
As weaknesses
Because, trust me, it's not easy to pass my test.
I'm a woman that is real,
And can turn anything into a meal

For you, me, and the whole family to eat.
I believe in building a foundation with substance
Along with romance,
With all the mechanisms that it takes to make you relive
every moment over and over again.
I'm that woman that is strong when you're weak,
Pick you up when you're down,
Your lawyer through your trials,
Your cheerleader even when you are losing.
I will love you, honor you, cherish you, respect you, nurture
you, and even obey you.
I don't know if you can see, but that's the woman that I am.

Josie Dorlus

I Read You Wrong

So good-looking, but underneath your hood is all garbage
Appeared to be the ideal man, but you're not even half that
Lazy, conceited, don't even have a clue who you are
All you want to do is screw left and right
And your game ain't even tight
At your age, you should be ashamed
But I'm sure you'll find someone to blame, though.
Your parents, society, the economy, unemployment... Please!
On top of it, you act like you got it figured out
Still have no idea where you're going
Thought you had potential
But when I checked your credentials, it's a no-go
But you got options though
Yeah, which length of skirt you're gonna get into next
Options like these will lead you to the roads of STDs
And when you get there, stay far away from me
'Cause I will be nowhere to be found.

To the One That I Love

I searched all over for you
I couldn't find you
I knew that there was such a thing
Called soul mate, my Eve, my queen
Little did I know that you were only
A prayer away.
On my knees, faithfully, I prayed for you
Waiting patiently for you
Asking that the Father would find you for me
And grant me you as my ultimate prize
I realized when you came into my life
That my prayers were answered
I love you with every fiber of my being
Without you, I am a man missing a rib
My love, my queen, my Eve
Be with me and make me whole again
With you, I can breathe better
With you, I reach higher
You complete me in so many ways
I wouldn't have it any other way
Then to spend the rest of my life with you
I love you....
Will you marry me?

Josie Dorlus

Not into You

❧

You meet someone
And the physical attraction is obvious
That's a good thing because
You need chemistry to proceed.
Conversation takes place
In your mind, you want to play hard to get
Then you thought,
"What the heck?
Maybe I'll cut to the chase."
Big mistake.
The chase is what keeps you in the game
It gives you the upper hand, ladies
Because nothing happens without your consent.
You let your guard down
Decided to keep an open mind
And hope that this one is one of a kind.
At first, there was excitement
On both ends, that is
But when you're not giving in
Time spent with you starts to diminish.
See, that's not being into you
Being into you means spending time with you
Being into you is wanting to get to know you
Not what's between your legs.

Courting you
Do what they say and say what they mean
There are twenty-four hours in a day
For someone who is so interested
That they can't find a minute to give you
Which you are worth more anyway
Clearly says that they're just not into you.

Josie Dorlus

I'm a Choice, Not an Option

When you look at me
All you see is sex
All you want is sex
There would be nothing with that
If you were my husband
But you're not.
Your actions say that you like me
Your words definitely want me
Yet you don't have time for me,
Except when you're thinking of getting laid.
You think it's cool to have multiple friends that way
Friends with benefits, that is.
See, there is something about me
That keeps you coming,
It's called the chase.
Little did you know you have no case
I will never make that mistake
To be with you while you're getting with everyone else.
All I know is you're all about having a good time
But you have noticed that I'm one of a kind
And, boy, does it blow your mind?
At times, you completely ignore me
Just to go get your needs met

Oh, but when I mentioned it, you get upset
Get over yourself
Your mind games don't phase me
I'm not about to waste my time
When you can't even make up your mind.
You need to make a decision
I'm a choice, not an option.

Josie Dorlus

I Love the Way You Love Me

In your eyes, I'm perfect just the way I am
So you said, therefore, I try my best to be that person.
From my hair, to my eyes, down to my size
Every time I want to change something
About myself, you gave me many reasons
Along with lectures why I shouldn't.
There is nothing that you won't do for me
You have been exactly what I needed and more
It's like I've never been loved like this before
It feels so good to be yours
The care you give to me can't be ignored.
I waited all my life to feel this way
I pray to God with me you'll stay
For us to grow and never be apart
Because I knew my heart was yours from the start
I love the way you love me.
Often, I asked myself if I deserve it
Still, you kept on loving me
How can I ever thank you for loving me so
Profoundly, unselfishly, freely, and unconditionally?
I am beyond grateful to have you in my life
And for that, I can't wait for you to be my wife
Because, baby, I love the way you love me.

Travelling Thoughts

Cruel Like That

What would you do
If somehow you knew I wasn't true to you?
How would you feel
If you caught me in a lie?
What would you say?
Would you listen to me while I explained,
Or would you leave 'cause you're tired of my lies?
What makes you think
That the things you do won't be coming back to you?
What would you say
If I were to play your games?
You would call me names,
Even worse, you'll make it look like I'm no good.
But it's okay, because I am tired anyway.
Well, how do you think I feel
When you call me her name by mistake,
When you tell her words that I want to hear,
When you're calling her name in your sleep?
How do you think I know
when you've been with her?
'Cause the way you smell.
When I'm all alone and you're having fun.
'Cause you're cruel like that.

Congratulations

‿❦‿❦‿

Work was hard, but you didn't complain
Not enough time, still you found a way
With dedication, motivation, and concentration
You felt obligated to finish your tasks.
Congratulations to a well deserved person
Who stopped at nothing and didn't let anything
Interrupt this beautiful day that has come forth.
Because of your endurance, today you are victorious
There is no doubt in my mind that you will
Prosper in everything you do.
So go and conquer the world
with the all the skills that God gave you.
Congratulations, you deserve the very best.

Josie Dorlus

Forgive Me, Father

೧ಲ⊶ರ⊷ಲಾ

Forgive me, Father, for I have sinned.
Forgive me for thinking that
you have forgotten me
Though your word says, "I will never leave you
or forsake you."
My flesh won't shut up
It just keeps talking
Oh, Father, forgive me
For letting my heart feel more
for other things, the worldly, earthly things
Instead of falling in love with you
more and more, Lord.
Forgive me for doubting your word,
the one that I should be relying on no matter what
But, Father, my heart wants to be so upset
for not having someone to *physically* mend it
I'm trying every day not to fail you,
but my thoughts keep giving me away
Father, let it rain on me,
the love you bestowed on many
Let it fall down on me too, yes, even me
Father, I know that it's in the spirit,
but let it manifest through and through

Until my body, my mind,
and my soul cry out yes to you, Lord.
I know that I know better, Father,
but please forgive my subconscious
So that consciously I know exactly who I am
and where I stand
Father, forgive me...

Josie Dorlus

My Cry

Many times, I called out to you
You don't answer
My heart is aching and full of rage
Where are you
as I'm going through these tough patches?
I'm asking how much more of this can I bear?
I know you see this, so please, do something
Save me from my sins
Spare me the hurt and the pain
Too many years have gone by,
and you've been silent
At least, show up one day for a moment
Give me a sign to know that you're there
For in my heart, I know that you are real
Give me yet another reason to believe
Birth in me the desire to be hopeful
Strengthen me with your love
that's unconditional
I'm on my knees,
pleading with you to give me another try
For only you can hear my cry.

Falling in Love with a Stranger

Remember on that day how strangely we met
By talking over the phone?
You touched a part of me
I wondered, "Could it be I'm falling for you?"
So here you are, here I am
It's too good to be true
There were times in my mind I felt you next to me
Feel so good, brought me tears
As you touched a part of me
I feel like at one time I knew of you before
So here you are, here I am,
love brought us through
I never thought that this day would come.
To fall in love with you on the telephone
I never thought it's possible
to love someone you've never seen.
And I fell in love with a stranger
And I could've been in danger
But, Lord, you knew that he was true
And I fell in love with a stranger
And it wasn't because I had hunger
But, Lord, you knew that he came from you
And only you.

Josie Dorlus

Something about You

You make me feel a certain way
That I can't even begin to explain
You move me just by the way you talk
And when you say hello, I can barely walk
There something about you, what is it?
Is it the way you look into my eyes?
Is it the way you hold my hand
to get my attention?
Is it your touch, your kiss,
or your warm embrace?
No one else has ever made me feel this way
I love the way I feel when I'm around you
You make me feel
like I'm the only one you see
You show me how much you're into me
The feeling that you bring
makes me wonder if there's more...
I want to find out
because there's definitely something about you.

The Resumé

Mocha is my complexion
Yes, I'm a woman of actions
Because to me, they do speak louder than words
To say the least, I know my worth
Details, they do matter
Analytical is what they call me
Soft-spoken, charismatic, and yes, I can be mean
I can be as sweet as candy
If you're diabetic, don't try me
At the same time,
this chic is as serious as a heart attack
To think that you can get me off track
Nah, it ain't happening like that
Conservationist, can be
Sassy, always; naughty, maybe
Honest and too outspoken
Something I'm still working on
Been independent far too long
So men think that I'm too strong
Not because we can't get along
Just the fact that I can hold my own
Strong character is what I'm after
Among other things especially laughter

Josie Dorlus

So I'm being transparent
No, it's not because I'm trying to be different
On the other hand, I am different
A queen who's searching for her king
To be qualified, you need experience in the field
Easy to please, long as it's coming from the heart
Teamwork is essential
Definitely have to have potential
Respectable, loyal, and honest is part of my list
Among other things to discuss when we meet
To love is my desire
To be in love is another....

Forbidden Fruits

The way she looks, the way she smiles
Makes you wonder, gosh, she's fine
When will it be?
How will it be when you make your move?
Something inside is saying no
But still you push and push to know
What really isn't your concern?
Because at home you have your own.
You find a way to meet her eyes
Purposely walking by her side.
Only to notice on her hand
The marking of another man.
Again, again you still insist
That you're the one she should be with.
What would it take to me? You see,
That this is not the fruit to eat.
If it's not yours, thou shalt not steal
And if she's married, thou shalt not want.

Josie Dorlus

Hello

Is there ever a time in your life
That you felt so low like you've hit the ground?
You wondering your purpose in this world
That you're standing in
And you wanna give in.
Just when a thought like that sets in,
Something happens that makes you smile.
But the feeling still exists,
And you wanna cry out.
I know you're feeling lost and all alone,
But you can't let go
'Cause you gotta win.
Just look ahead a little more,
And you'll see the light
That was always within.
Hold on to the words that you see
What doesn't kill you makes you strong
And the victory is yours
And you'll wanna cry out
You don't need to give in to your fears
Stay away from the negatives
Should you fall off, get back up again
Don't worry about what people say

They will say something anyway
Should you fall off, get back up again
Hello, is there anybody out there
who can relate?

Josie Dorlus

The Day

Far away
But yet so near
Can't believe the day is almost here
For us to meet
To see the face, and match the voice
Under the stars just you and me
Gazing into each others' eyes.
At last, chemistry
That's so surreal
Will have a chance to learn a new dance,
new steps...
Yes, I know you're far away,
Can't wait to see you in two days...

Happy Birthday

Today is your birthday
And it's your day to celebrate
Be grateful and thank God for today
Tomorrow is another day
Life goes on anyway
I'm asking God to be with you
And bring you many more birthdays
I am happy to celebrate your new beginnings
With you
Enjoy it; kick up your heels if you have to
You can cry if you want to, just let it be
Tears of joy and not sorrows
Tomorrow is not promised to us
So eat right, live right, and keep being
The awesome human being that you are.
Happy birthday!

Josie Dorlus

Congrats

ભ્ય૰ભ્ય૰

Through all your hard work, you made it
Through the storms, you hung in there
Though there may have been sleepless nights
and lonely days,
You never let anything get in the way
And I always knew that you could do it
Congratulations on all your accomplishments
May you achieve all your heart's desires
Just wanted you to know that I'm proud of you
It's a big world out there
And it is waiting for you to make a difference
Congratulations!

Talk to Me

You've been so sad, you've been so far away
Is there something that's on your mind
that you care to talk about?
I'm here for you when you need someone
To be your friend, let me hold your hand
I'm trying to figure out
What exactly is wrong with you?
Lately, you're sad and so distant
When I ask you what is going on
You're not talking, you're not saying a thing
Whenever I would try to work it out
Like a good woman should
You pull away and walk away
I know something has changed
Whenever you need me, I will be there
To be the one to comfort you
And everything you need and more
You know, baby, you can tell me anything
My arms are wide open
So why don't you talk to me?
From the look in your eyes,
I can tell something is wrong, baby
When I ask you, you don't want to tell me

Josie Dorlus

How exactly can we work this out?
If you're not talking
You're saying a lot of things.

You're Worth It

ᒐᕈᕈᔕ

Ever since you came into my life
Things have changed for the better
Ever since you came into my life, I am happier
I remember how hard it was to admit
that I needed you
I remember how I felt when I couldn't see you
Many times, all I wanted to know
Was that you're okay
But there were so many obstacles in the way
I cried and prayed to the Lord above
To give me someone I can love
Someone my heart will always want
Someone my eyes will only see
The fight I fought just to have you
The pain I bear waiting for you, only to win you
It didn't matter what I went through
As long as God sent you
Which confirms that I was meant to have you
To know that you're one of a kind
And hope one day that you'll be mine
Now, here you are right in my arms
After so many years have gone by
You looked at me, and then, we smiled
I have to say that you're worth it

Josie Dorlus

Losing Mama

Never thought the day would come
That I would have to say good-bye to my mom
The first woman in my life
And I had no choice but to say good-bye
Never thought this day would come
When I would feel so alone
With no one to call my own
Mama, you tried and tried so hard
For us to never be apart
But it was out of our hands
For reasons that I will never understand
I guess it was all God's plan
To watch you fighting for your health
Until you took your last breath
The hardest thing I had to do
Was to say good-bye to my best friend
Loving you was the best thing
And in my heart that will never end
I miss you, Mama…

Happy Anniversary

⚬⚬⚬⚬⚬

Who would've thought we would make it this far?
I had no idea that I would be this blessed
To have you by my side for all those years
To love, honor, and cherish just like we promised
Those promises came from my heart to yours
You have been my best friend, my lover,
and my wife all in one
I couldn't ask for a better person
To have an anniversary with you every year is a gift
I promise to continue loving you
more and more each day
For you were chosen to be mine
I will spend the rest of my life appreciating you,
showing you how much I love you
And making sure that you never regret choosing me
Agreeing with me is not easy sometimes
But you make it so easy to be a good person
Though we chose this particular day to celebrate
In my heart, every day is an anniversary with you.
I love to love you.
Happy Anniversary, my love.

Happy Father's Day

രearly

If you could have it your way
I know you would choose to be a full-time dad
But the circumstances of life
changes the status of things
The reality is that in your heart and soul you work
As a full-time daddy all year around
No matter what words that are spoken
and how certain situations make you feel
Remember that God could've chosen anyone else
To be a dad to this beautiful child
He chose you. I'm not sure where life
will take you and me
But I was sent to remind you
On this very day that only
you could've been this child's father
You were chosen because of your
heart, passion, courage, and gentle spirit
This child is not only blessed,
but also lovingly blessed to have you as a dad
Enjoy this day of many to come,
and smile like others do
I'm sure you are pictured as super dad,
and that's good enough to make you smile.
Happy father's day!

God Gained an Angel Today

೧ະ⊙ະⓍ⊙ะ⊙

It doesn't make sense how it's over
You can't understand why it's over
Here today, and gone tomorrow
Your heart is filled with so much sorrow
You don't know where to begin to understand
How all of this can come to an end
But remember the joy, remember the laughs
That their presence brought into your lives
Remember the touch, remember the words
Only an angel could've spoken
The pain you feel is true indeed
For God alone knows how you feel
To turn your loss into his gain
Is something God can only explain.
The fact that he gained and angel today…
My condolences…

Dedicated to Maria Martinez

Josie Dorlus

Something in the Spirit:
A Personal Note

∽≈⊙≈∽

Have you ever met someone, and for some reason, there is something about their spirit that doesn't sit right with yours? It's not a matter of being judgmental because we shouldn't judge anyone—that's God's job. As you get close to God, this goes without saying. When you ask God for discernment, align yourself to be in the position to receive it, for it is very precious and remarkable.

Many times, we can identify a lying, sad, or mean spirit. We can point those out based on someone's words and or actions. Nevertheless, pay attention when something in your spirit moves. Communicate with God to understand what that means. There are things that come to your spirit that won't leave you until you understand them and are putting them to work. Here is an opinion that I want to share about something in the spirit. Let's take a single woman who has been praying for God to send her a husband, like I did. The decision is made to accept applications, as far as dating is concerned. As you begin to date, you notice that the applicants are not much to your liking, and some of them you know for sure are not God-sent. As time goes by, some of us begin to lower our standards, which is not always a recommendation in my book. As you pray for God to send you someone that he hand picked for you, he will do that. The problem we face is the waiting period. While we wait, it's easy to get tempted, impatient, and discouraged to the point that we begin to settle for someone that is not from God and that is not worthy of our love.

Some spirits are uninvited and very sneaky. At the same time, if you pay close attention, there is a trail to follow. One of the most uninvited spirits is procrastination. It is also a smart spirit. It recognizes potential, greatness, and strength. Notice that when you're up to something good, and especially if it's something that pleases God, that's when you're feeling lazy, tired, restless, not even able to start what's in your heart. You keep putting things off and/or avoiding the subject. You find excuses after excuses not to get started or not to finish. I'm talking about it because I allow that spirit to lease a room in the chambers of my heart. Little did I know that the spirit didn't want to lease anymore; it wanted to own me.

Procrastination is like cancer. It's undetectable, and the symptoms are not noticeable until it costs you something or it's too late. We all have different ways of dealing with spirits. The important thing is to know how to deal and overcome them. I chose that spirit to talk about because it delayed the writing of this book. I've learned that nothing happens without God and his timing is the best. At times, we won't understand what takes him so long to do what he is doing, but the key is trust and relying on him always.